Wooden Ships; Iron Man

William Mangan

BookLocker
Trenton, Georgia

Table of Contents

Preface

History is derived from many sources. Cave drawings, archeological findings, hieroglyphics, eyewitness accounts, auto biographies, piecing together events, forensic investigations, videotaping, voice recording, just to name a few. But basically, the keystone, the historic method comes from human verbal communication and discourse. Relating events through speech.

My maternal grandfather, Lorenz Anton Ludvig Laatz is not a historical figure. Basically, he would be considered a normal ordinary German-American immigrant who married an American citizen and raised five kids. But much of his life was far from ordinary. In fact, he traveled the world and had adventures that most folks only dream of or see in movies. And this was in the first thirty years of his life.

How do I know? Because I was the recipient of him telling about his adventures and life, and this, pieced together with other evidence forms a pretty good picture of his history. He had no reason to embellish the stories he related to me. He was matter of fact. He had an engineering mind and I never detected a big ego. I don't believe he transmitted this much information to anyone else. Somehow we had a connection and he felt comfortable telling me. He died when I was seventeen, but I spent a lot of my life visiting him. He was my mentor and my hero.

The stories and adventures that form the meat of his history emulate from my personal memory as I recall him telling me. Therefore, it is undoubtedly not perfect, but I have a pretty good recollection and will do my best to relate accurately.

The stories he told me had no timeline, per se. They were told because of something that jarred his memory. It could have been a National Geographic magazine, a newspaper article, something on TV, or another source. Many times he would illustrate something in the story. He liked to draw and was pretty good at it. Sometimes it could be a memento that he had kept, such as a dagger that he acquired after a man tried to stab him. I still have that dagger.

But years later, when traveling to his home town in Germany, I obtained from relatives still living there, postcards that he sent home from whatever part of the world he was in. They gave these postcards to me. They are dated, and have a picture of his location as he traveled around the world. So I will try to match the stories with the timeline established by the postcards. He never gave a return address though. It turns out that one of the reasons for his departure at age eighteen was apparently to escape being drafted into Kaiser Wilhelm's Army! This is something I never knew until my visit. It seems he harbored some subsequent paranoia that haunted him:

could he be tracked down and punished for eluding service to his Kaiser?

Even when he finally married an American and established a family in Seattle, Washington State, his first child, my mother, was born in 1916, there was still some fear. Why? WW I was beginning and Germans living in the U.S.A. were sometimes eyed with skepticism relative to their allegiance, especially if they belonged to German immigrant organizations. He did and it could be scary. There actually were some German spies lurking about that were apprehended by U.S. government agents. He was still careful about mailings to his family still in Deutschland, so refrained from including a return address.

He belonged to a German fraternal club: The Sons of Hermann. As a child my mother would accompany him to some of their dinner meetings. She learned much about his home country and culture. This influenced her into corresponding with the family in Germany and we do still to this day, now by email. But he also was a Mason...not a German club. Most of all though, he was a proud, patriotic American demonstrated by an American Flag tattooed on his arm. He loved America and never returned to his homeland. Neither did my mother or any of his other four children. But I did...years later...and not only paid a visit to his home city, but the actual house in which he was raised! It was a spiritual experience. I felt his presence. Whether this was only imagined, I don't know. I only know that I felt it.

So here is the story of an authentic adventurer.

Chapter 1:
Grandpa Laatz

I recall laying on his belly falling asleep. He always wore a dress shirt, tie, and carried a pocket watch. He smelled like cigars or a pipe… never smoked cigarettes. He shaved with a straight razor and splashed on cologne or aftershave which smelled good. On his upper sleeves were arm garters that kept his long shirtsleeves at just the right length at the wrist. He wore slacks of some sort held up with suspenders because his butt was skinny. I never saw him in jeans. He had big, tough strong hands, with tough looking fingernails. He would tickle me on top of the knee with his index fingernail driving me crazy. I've never seen anyone else that could do that.

If I coaxed him, sometimes he would roll up his sleeves and show me his tattoos. Some of the colors were fading. One was an American flag with a great eagle. I loved it. He also had an anchor with rope around it. He could flex his bicep and make it jump. I loved that too. But the best of all was to see him wiggle his little finger stump where a falling chunk of coal had taken it off at the middle joint while loading coal into a ship. We would both laugh.

He had many missing teeth from contracting scurvy in his twenties, but seeing a dentist was out of the question. His wife, my grandma, had false teeth that looked nice. But not him…

no way. So when he smoked a cigar, which was often, he could hold it in one of the spaces in his mouth. He would dip things in his coffee or other drinks to make it easier to chew. He liked his coffee with cream and sugar. Sometimes I'd get a taste.

At home, I hated tomatoes, but he got me to eat them with a little sugar and coaxing. It drove my mother crazy.

She'd say: "You be a good boy and eat those tomatoes."

I'd stare at the tomatoes, wishing I was at grandpas, and kind of whine: "but grandpa puts sugar on them."

"Well," she'd reply, "we don't do that in this house."

Fortunately, my dog would eat tomatoes! I'd slip them under the table.

Mom was his daughter. He had been strict with his own kids and she carried the torch. She was the daily enforcer in our house for most issues. But sometimes I'd hear, "just wait until your father gets home." That was the heavy artillery. Then you'd sweat for hours! Waiting. But actually, when Dad finally arrived, I think all he wanted to do was relax and have a beer. He would kiss her and she'd settle down. So usually the waiting was worse than the final hammer.

I liked to watch him shave. In the bath was a corner sink, the mirror hanging tilted above, the bottom two corners each resting on wall molding, the top by a chain. He salvaged that mirror from a big sailing ship. I still have it. He would let me help mix the soap in a mug, get it all foamy with steaming water from the stove kettle and then slop it on his face. He would finish up around his mouth and nose like he was an artist painting a picture, just right. Then he would paint my face the same. Very carefully he'd stroke his straight razor on the leather strop hanging from the wall, to freshen it up, then begin shaving. I could hear the rasping sound of the razor on the whiskers. Then he would dip into the sink washing the blade in the remaining hot kettle water, swishing into the glop of whiskers and cream that formed in the sink. No water running, faucets off until time to wash the sink. Concurrently, I'd emulate his moves with my dummy razor. I had a little mirror down low. Very carefully we would get it done then towel off. He would let me feel his face. Smooth. Me too. Then we'd splash on after shave, both smelling wonderful for the ladies!

Then came the hair. He had some glop in a jar that was the viscosity of syrup. He would dip his comb into it and blend it into his hair, then mine. He would make a part, comb the side down and then kind of swirl the widest section. It would dry that way and stiffen. Actually, I never really cared for the style, but tolerated it for his sake.

He shopped at the Pike Place Market, an open market of all varieties of fruits, vegetables, meats, breads, sweets, pig brains

… anything edible. In addition, there were vendors of books, Army Navy Surplus, Salvation Army, Good Will, nick knacks, smoking supplies, used and new clothes, pets, household items, tricks, and local artists hawking their wares. He went about once a week. When I was old enough, I went with him. Standing straight looking level, I saw grandpa's pants above the knee. One time I lost track of his pants and panicked. He found me and gave me a hug.

We would catch the trolley to town. He would be dressed in a shirt, tie, vest, suit or sport coat, and always a hat. Most men wore a hat then. My father wore his with the brim rolled down in front, but grandpa left his the same as the sides and back. He always kept his shoes shined. That was a big deal. We would shine mine too. He would finish with liquid at the sole edges. This was the sign of a groomed man. We'd walk to the bus stop and I'd hold his hand on the way. The trolley always smelled like other people. I'd watch them and sometimes doze to the monotonous sound and vibration of the bus.

The smells of the market were incredible. They made me hungry. The butcher at his favorite meat market always gave me a little wiener. I ate it raw. We always stopped by Woolworth's Department Store. There, the popcorn smell dominated, but his favorite purchase was a coffee and a hot dog, which was so hot, I couldn't bite into it. So I waited for mine to cool while watching him devour his with lots of mustard. He must have had a steel mouth! Same with the steaming hot coffee, although tempered with cream. I can't recall what I drank. Maybe a Coke.

He always saved his shopping bags. They were big with strong corded paper handles. He'd carry them folded under his arm on the way to the market and stuffed full returning. He invented a wooden handle that tucked under the cord handle to alleviate digging into his hands. We would unload the groceries and smell the aromas in the process. He loved cheese, especially the stinky stuff like limburger, or meats like liver worst. I couldn't partake, but he could talk me into at least tasting. He would look at me and laugh as my palate revolted. But one thing we would eat together was raw hamburger, red onion, salt and pepper on thin rye. Yummy! He would cook fried pig's feet with German style potatoes and a vegetable. Also yummy!

He bought me little turtles at the pet store. Usually one, but I recall having two at certain times. I would have turtle races at home on the kitchen vinyl floor. I kept them in a little terrarium and fed them bugs. One morning I went to fetch them and one wouldn't move. I was baffled. I told mom and she said it was dead. I had no idea what dead meant. I said we could take it to grandpa and he could probably fix it. She explained dead to me the best she could and we ended up wrapping the turtle in a napkin and burying it in the back yard. I made a cross out of popsicle sticks. We said prayers. Periodically I would visit the gravesite and imagine my little turtle in the dirt. Of course, it happened again with other turtles and then birds that I would find. We had a regular cemetery in our backyard.

As I grew older, grandpa would buy me other things. Sometimes when I was with him and sometimes on his own, followed by a phone call to mom that he needed to see me because he had something. Then I couldn't wait to get there and see. He would always make me wait a little. I kept my mouth shut. When he was ready, he'd go in the back room and bring it out. I would be mesmerized while he explained how it worked or the significance of it. He didn't say it was mine until after he was sure I was enamored. Only then would he say just two words: "take it." I would be thrilled. He loved my reaction.

Some of the items he gave me were: wooden skis with the bindings that absolutely locked your feet in, ski boots made of leather, a long bow made of Yew wood with some arrows, an authentic Marine Corps combat knife with sheath, a WWII canteen, G.I. belt (the kind with all the metal holes for attaching stuff), an M-1 training rifle, a bomber airplane headset (earphones) with a microphone that plugged into something on a plane, an Army jacket, a Navy officer's hat and other men stuff.

Sometimes we'd make a kite and fly it at the park where there were no wires. He explained what happened to Edison flying his kite in a storm. I certainly didn't want to touch any wires. Ouch!

At night, we would walk outside and look at the sky. He recognized every planet, every constellation and the names of many stars. He called Venus, We-ness---his German. The sailors of his day navigated by knowing the stars.

He taught me how to tie knots, replete with their name. Square knot, bowline, clove hitch, bowline on a bite, hangman's noose, etc., then he taught me how to splice line. The eye splice, end splice, joiner splice. Then some macramé like a Turks head, a monkey fist, various braiding and such. He could make mats and do all kinds of rope yarn work. We were always going to make a ship-in-a-bottle, but never got to it before he died.

He made a drawing of the different sailing vessel types. Each mast length and location designates a specific vessel. Included are the number of sails, each with a name.

He was a self-taught electrician and showed me how to wire a lamp or change out a wall receptacle. Instruction was given on the theory of electricity, amps, current, circuits and hot to ground.

When I turned sixteen, I began working on ferryboats. My father was a Puget Sound ferryboat Captain as was his father. Grandpa would call me a "Jackshite" and laugh like mad. I never figured out what that meant, but suspect it was something like a flunky piss ant deck hand just learning the marine environment working on boats. I didn't care because I knew he loved and was proud of me.

He knew about body building way before anyone else. Even back when he was working on big wooden ships, he would lift weights and do resistance training. Of course, back then, around the late 1890's and early 1900's, there were no body building products like today, so they had to improvise. But he knew how to build muscle. He wasn't a tall man, only about 5'7", but in his prime was fit, strong and quick. He worked out.

So when I reached about ten to twelve years old, he would give me magazine articles about bodybuilding. There was a man named Charles Atlas (Angelo Siciliano 1892-1972) that advertised his method. He called it Dynamic Tension. Charles had a fine physic and the ladies liked him a lot. They showed cartoons of a wimpy, skinny guy getting sand kicked in his face, then six months later, after following the methods of Charles, he was transformed into a muscled up, kick ass guy that returned to the bully and straightened him out. Grandpa wanted to make sure I followed that path. And I did, ending up playing college football, rugby and becoming a martial artist. My parents had no clue … grandpa did.

Into my teenage years I definitely grew interested in girls, but my parents put the kibosh on dating and parties. I did play sports. But since I didn't date, I would get out of the house by visiting grandpa on Friday or Saturday night, sometimes both. He would be there usually by himself because my grandma was a babysitter for some families. I would usually walk the mile to their house.

Inside the front door, the top third of the living room was a cloud of smoke, usually cigar, but occasionally a pipe. He smoked crappy cigars, but the pipe tobacco was nice, sweet and aromatic. It was a short walk to the couch, covered with a large hand knitted quilt, brightly colored. Grandpa sat on the left end, next to his smoking table, in which were his cigars, pipes, cans of tobacco and always the same ashtray. He had several hatpins three to four inches long used to impale a cigar's last inch so he could smoke it to the nubbins. Sometimes he would crack open a window or the door to let smoke escape. To the right of the door, in the corner of the room was the black and white TV set. We would watch several westerns in succession or wrestling. The wrestling was staged of course, but didn't seem as phony as today. Sometimes they would really hurt each other. They were good athletes. Other programs we liked were animal or history shows. Sometimes comedy, like Red Skelton.

Sometimes we'd play cards, usually cribbage. He would boil water in the kettle and we'd have coffee or tea and some of grandma's cookies.

But it was on that couch where he recounted his stories and adventures, many times using a paper tablet to illustrate. For example, to draw the shape of the ax head used by the African chief to kill a lion. We would even splice line sitting there.

He recounted his adventures and told me about sharks, whales, lions, elephants, birds, sea creatures, astronomy, ships, fights he got in, foods he had eaten, people he had met and how he felt.

For instance, at one time he was the ship's carpenter. One of the crew came around and using a knife, began cutting a notch into grandpa's new work bench…Lord knows why. Grandpa then asked the crewman if he could see the knife, so it was handed over. Grandpa proceeded to drive it through the crewman's jacket that he had laid down. Indignant, the crewman asked, "why on earth did you do that?" Grandpa answered, "why did you carve up my new workbench?"

End of story.

Chapter 2:
Going to Sea

Here I was in Lubeck, Germany, the birthplace of Grandpa. It is April of the year 1996. I am walking around by myself reflecting on the city. My wife was back at the hotel. My son was staying with relatives. I am experiencing a rather eerie feeling. Is it just my perception, or is my grandpa's spirit near? It can't be proven, but I know I felt something. It became so strong I teared up. I walked the waterfront where there were wooden vessels berthed. I was smoking a Cuban. I imagined grandpa here as a child running around wide eyed and adventurous.

Lubeck, old town, is a giant fort of brick exterior walls, built in a circular fashion on an island that split's the Trave River which runs into the Baltic Sea, so the city is surrounded by water like a moat, which is probably what Adolf II, the Count of Schauenburg and Holstein had in mind in 1143 when he established a settlement and built a castle. In 1181 it became an Imperial City. Emperor Barbossa soon ordained that it should have a ruling council of 20, which stuck until the 19th century. In 1375, Emperor Charles IV named Lubeck one of the five "Glories of the Empire" a title shared with Venice, Rome, Pisa, and Florence. It has always been a trading city, dominated by merchants. bib. 1

But evidently also a religious city, because inside the walls it is dominated by seven churches with towering steeples. They are beautiful brick gothic structures with stunning columns supporting numerous giant arches inside. Stained glass, sculpture, paintings, and spiritual iconic trim work prevail. Near the edge walls are crypts of big church donors who apparently thought they could buy their way to heaven. Truly impressive and mystical, built beginning in the middle ages. But even Sacred Heart Church, built in 1888, blends in architecturally. bib. 2

Besides the churches there are breathtaking old buildings: a hospital, town hall, giant houses, row houses and restaurants. All retaining a medieval appearance amid winding, narrow, cobblestone streets. In the city center is a large area designed for a vibrant open market constantly bristling with activity.

For several centuries, Lubeck was the "capital of the Hanseatic League, a medieval guild, a trade organization. Today it is listed by UNESCO as a World Heritage Site. bib. 3

In WWII, the city was the first German city to be attacked in substantial numbers by the Royal Air Force causing severe damage to the historic center and several of the majestic churches. It has taken years to repair and is still not completely restored. I see unrepaired damage now, in 1996. bib. 4

Lorenz Anton Ludvig Laatz, my grandpa, was born May 27, 1883. He was one of eight children by parents Johann Ludvig Laatz and Marie Beck. His twin sister Emma died at age two. The Laatz's were gardeners. Their first farmhouse, built by Lorenz's grandfather, Heinrich Ernst Laatz, still stands west of old Lubeck, now owned by a religious group.

However Lorenz grew up living in the city in a large townhouse type structure. I am shown this place on my visit. But he definitely was taught gardening. I recall all the trees and plants he grew in his yard and house in Seattle. He had a green thumb.

So his childhood was a variety of chores, school, large close family, loving siblings and no doubt many adventures and antics. He reminisced to me most about church and school.

Most all of the churches in Lubeck are Lutheran. But he spoke of the strictness of Nuns, slapping or switching on his hands at school. In addition, he spoke of being an altar boy. This is Catholic. But of what church? Sacred Heart Church was built in 1888 when Lorenz was five years old, so this must have been the one. It was Roman Catholic. In Seattle, he and grandma married in St. James Cathedral, a Catholic Church and their family was raised Catholic, attending St. Edwards Church. This was passed on to me. I attended St. Mary's Church.

Lorenz was Nordic in appearance, fair features, blond hair, piercing blue grey eyes, lean and trim, 5'7" tall, big hands and fairly slim face. He must have had fun growing up in an area so vibrant and diverse.

All around was water, since the Trave River flowed around the city with portions formed into canals. Consequently there are many bridges. There are lakes, parks, gardens and an avenue lined with gnarled lime trees planted in 1814. Eleven miles to the north the Trave empties into the Baltic Sea with flat sandy beaches which today is a giant seaside resort, Travemunde. In those days, boat travel was the primary method of moving goods. The market place bristled with activity. Given this scenario, it is amazing that Lorenz never learned how to swim!

As Lorenz moved into his teenage years, he apparently harbored visions of the world at large. He was smart and alert and probably heard stories from travelers about far off places. He was creative and a dreamer evidenced by the poems that he authored later in his life of which I now possess. He was a thinker. He also liked the concept of personal freedom. Being raised Catholic with its dogma and nuns cracking his knuckles and slapping with switches did not suit him well. So when he felt Kaiser Wilhelm II knocking on his door either directly or figuratively, he figured he would make a break.

Friedrich Wilhelm Vicktor Albert was Germany's last Emperor, or Kaiser. His father was Prince Frederick William of Prussia. His mother was Victoria, Princess Royal, daughter of Britain's queen Victoria. Ascending to the throne in 1888, he was commonly called Kaiser Wilhelm II. His predecessor was Frederick III.

Kaiser Wilhelm II was trained in the military and when crowned was described as bellicose, bombastic and impetuous. In 1890 he dismissed the German Chancellor, Otto von Bismarck who was a peacemaker and negotiator.

The Kaiser embarked on a "New Course" for Germany in foreign affairs that culminated in his support for Austria-Hungary in the crisis of 1914 which led in a matter of days to the First World War. He eventually abdicated in 1918 and fled into exile in the Netherlands. bib. 5

But in 1888 Lorenz would be five years old. It's unknown how much understanding a child of five would have, but by 1893, at age ten, he may have had more. In those days, a boy became a man about thirteen or fourteen, at least be trained into a profession and put to work. It's feasible he could have been "feeling the heat" relative to his future. One possibility would have been getting drafted in the good old Kaiser's army!

His brother Heinrich indeed was inducted into the Army. Some of Lorenz's later post cards were addressed to him in Berlin where his barracks were in the Bluncherstrasse.

***

Hamburg, Germany is 40-50 miles from Lubeck and was a major seaport city. Lorenz somehow made it there and hired on as a merchant sailor. The ship's name was the Erata. She was a three masted full rigger, one of many German ships plying the oceans at that time. They headed south and west. It's undetermined whether she made ports on the eastern U.S. or exactly where else, but she was headed for San Francisco. There was no Panama Canal yet. Its construction began in 1903 and wasn't completed until 1914 so they had to sail around Cape Horn, the southern tip of South America.

Grandpa kept a certificate, which I have, written in German, commemorating his passing over the Equator. It is dated 24 December 1901. It is framed in two parts. The top is the original in German, the bottom is the English translation. It reads:

> *Me Neptune, god of the ocean and ruler of all seas, rivers, swamps and marshes, states that the ordinary sailor Lorenz A. Laatz from Lubeck, received on this day of our Lord, December, 24th, 1901 the customary Christening while crossing the Line, and has the privilege from now on to sail on all the oceans, seas, etc., in ships, boats, or in whatever there is able to float or swim.*
>
> *Given under my Royal*

Seal and Signature.

NEPTUNE

It is signed by 3 witnesses, the Captain's yeoman and the Captain. (German version follows this chapter)

He would have been 18 years old at that line crossing since his birthdate was 5/27/83. Assuming this was his first line crossing, he must have signed on the Erata at age 18.

***

Every ship's crew must have a bully, so it stands to reason there was at least one provocateur on the Erato.

Grandpa was not a big man. He had blonde hair and a lean physique. But he was quick and tough, proud and resolute. So when a big bully on his ship began testing and provoking him he arranged a fistfight later in the day after evening chow so they could have it out. When chowtime came, Lorenz didn't show up.

This led to chatter among the crew and much blustering from the bully suggesting this was an indication of fear from his victim. The bully enjoyed his meal amid much braggadocio.

Sometime after dinner they met, apparently in a safe section of the ship. It's assumed there was an ample audience and some wagering. Lorenz's strategy was simple: be quick, elusive, and hit hard. Hit hard where? In the solar plexus and stomach of course! After all, the big guy had eaten a good meal not long before and Lorenz had not. So…bam-bam…move…pop-pop…wham, hard hits to the belly. Slight, lean man with strong, quick twitch muscles; big thick hands.

They say "it's not the size of the dog in the fight, but the size of the fight in the dog." I heard it didn't take long before the big guy was hurt bad…probably puking his guts out. Then a couple shots to the jaw and nose…and it was all over. So much for getting picked on!

***

Apparently they sailed down around the Horn and north to San Francisco. There is no evidence where or if they stopped along the way. "Around the Horn" actually means threading through the Strait of Magellan, a passage just north of the actual Horn, known for its brutal weather with strong winds, tides, rip currents and choppy wave action. In later years he would experience a significant storm that damaged his ship. He actually lost some belongings overboard.

Grandpa wrote in 1920 that the Erata departed San Francisco mid April 1902. Heading south, it took three months to get to Cape Horn, threading it on July 23, specifically at 12:30 AM. From there they headed north with I presume some stops along the way because it took six months to get to England.

He wrote they "could not make Falmouth" (don't know why), so went to Queenstown for orders later part of October." Queenstown is now Cobh, Ireland. The name was changed in the 1920's. It is located on the south coast of Ireland. From there, early November, they sailed to Newcastle on Thyne, which is on the east coast of England. By November 15, he wrote, the ship was back in Hamburg, Germany.

But certainly not to stay. It's doubtful he even paid a visit to Lubeck, especially if he was evading the draft, but it's possible. He had a taste of living on an ocean going sailing ship and evidently loved the life, so there was nothing more to do but sign on another ship and continue traveling, which he did for the next twelve years.

The names of all the various ships on which he served are lost, but his travels took him to West Africa and then North America and on to the Western Pacific. He made it to Singapore, but it doesn't appear he went through the Mediterranean Sea or Suez Canal to get there.

More on that later.

He was not a big drinker. He kept his wits about him. But he did encounter health issues. Over this time in these climates, he contracted scurvy from lack of vitamin C, malaria and most likely some other minor illnesses. Later in his life the effects of scurvy caused him to lose most of his teeth. My mother remembers him getting fever and sweats from the malaria still in his body. It never leaves.

He studied and learned and moved up in the ranks as a sailor, eventually becoming a ship's officer. He knew all the types of sails, rigging, macramé, carpentry, weather patterns and trends. They navigated by the stars using a sextant, dead reckoning and following the wind. They had the best charts of the day. He had freedom. The world was his oyster. He got some tattoos.

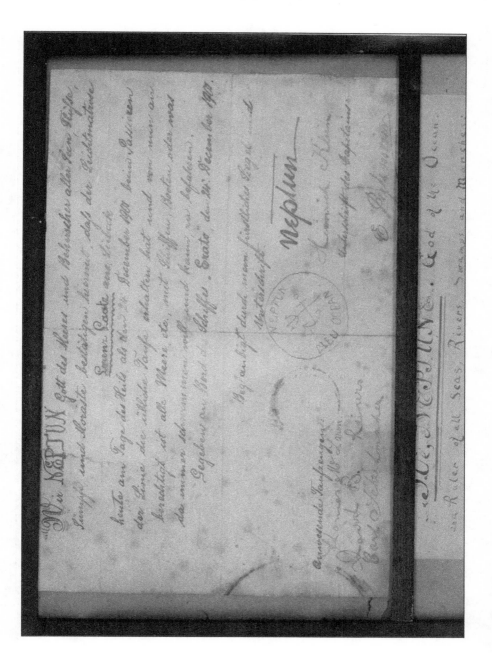

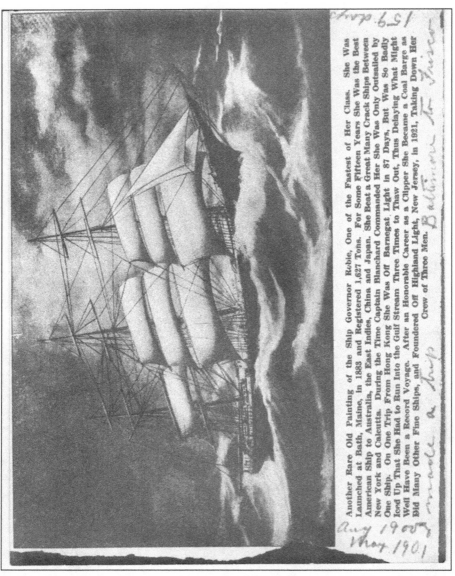

Another Rare Old Painting of the Ship Governor Robie, One of the Fastest of Her Class. She Was Launched at Bath, Maine, in 1883 and Registered 1,627 Tons. For Some Fifteen Years She Was the Best American Ship to Australia, the East Indies, China and Japan. She Beat a Great Many Crack Ships Between New York and Calcutta. During the Time Captain Blanchard Commanded Her She Was Only Outsailed by One Ship. On One Trip From Hong Kong She Was Off Barnegat Light in 87 Days, But Was So Badly Iced Up That She Had to Run Into the Gulf Stream Three Times to Thaw Out, Thus Delaying What Might Well Have Been a Record Voyage. After an Honorable Career as a Clipper She Became a Coal Barge as Did Many Other Fine Ships, and Foundered Off Highland Light, New Jersey, in 1921, Taking Down Her Crew of Three Men.

Robie is very similar to the Erata.

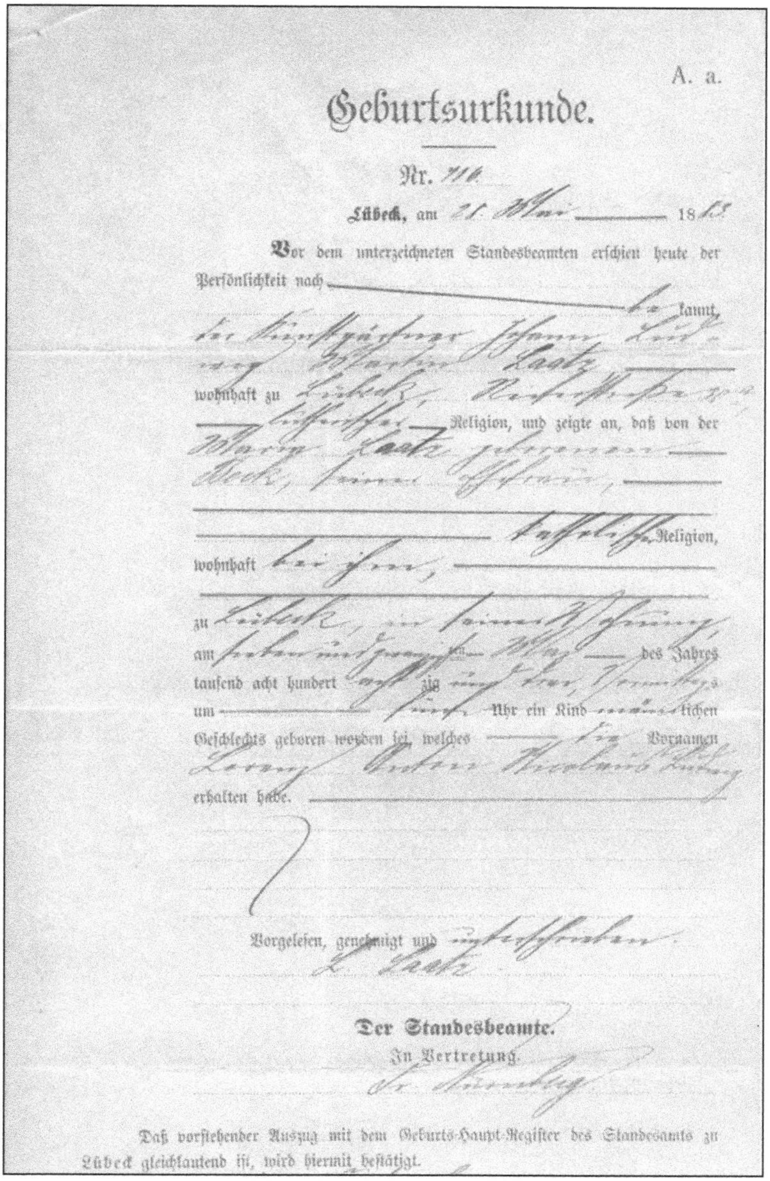

A. a.

Geburtsurkunde.

Nr. 710.

Lübeck, am 21. Mai 1883

Vor dem unterzeichneten Standesbeamten erschien heute der Persönlichkeit nach bekannt,

der Kunstgärtner Johann Ludwig Martin Laatz

wohnhaft zu Lübeck,

lutherischer Religion, und zeigte an, daß von der Maria Laatz geborene Beck, seiner Ehefrau,

katholischer Religion,

wohnhaft bei ihm,

zu Lübeck, in seiner Wohnung

am siebenundzwanzigsten Mai des Jahres tausend acht hundert achtzig und drei, Vormittags um fünf Uhr ein Kind männlichen Geschlechts geboren worden sei, welches die Vornamen Lorenz Anton Nicolaus Ludwig erhalten habe.

Vorgelesen, genehmigt und unterschrieben.
L. Laatz

Der Standesbeamte.
In Vertretung.
Dr. Nürnberg

Daß vorstehender Auszug mit dem Geburts-Haupt-Register des Standesamts zu Lübeck gleichlautend ist, wird hiermit bestätigt.

Lorenz Laatz birth certificate

Lubeck

Lorenz Laatz. Age 15. Lubeck, Germany

Chapter 3:
Adventures Just Beginning

It's unclear just when Lorenz headed for Africa and on what ship, but he signed on to a ship headed there. It must have been in his first years going to sea because after that the postcards are sent from North America and the western Pacific Ocean.

Somewhere along Africa's west coast near the Congo River, Yellow Fever broke out among the crew.

Yellow fever is a virus contracted through a mosquito bite. It is endemic to the Congo basin area of Africa. It affects the liver and causes jaundice whereby the skin turns yellow. There is no cure to this day although there is a vaccination now, unavailable in the early 1900's. Even today it kills 30,000 people each year, 90% in Africa. bib. 6

The ship was quarantined as a result. Lorenz may have caught it and suffered a mild case, or not, but he wound up surviving. Apparently, there were many that died. I hesitate to quote the numbers because I can't recall for sure. But the ship was subsequently burned. Knowledge of viruses back then was limited compared to today, so this was their solution.

But now Lorenz was stranded and out of a job. So, he applied and was hired running a boat on the Congo River. It must have been a steamboat since these were in service then. Either wood or coal fired heating a boiler connected to gears which turned a paddlewheel at the stern. The length could have been up to 50' I would imagine. It would have a shallow draft even though the Congo is a very deep river in places.

He carried supplies upriver and probably some products back down. It's not known how far upriver he went, but he described passing under tree branches extending out over the river where he would feed monkeys who were slumming for snacks. It was kind of a reverse zoo. I asked him if he was fearful of local natives that would do him harm…his reply was no because he would bring them gifts like mirrors, clay pipes, knives, or whatever he deemed they would enjoy. He was no threat, but rather a friend. He said their dislike and distrust was toward the missionaries who tried to change their lives and influence their customs and yes, this sometimes led to violent encounters.

One particular tribal chief especially took a shine to Lorenz. Maybe it was his blonde German hair and blue eyes. His tribe were lion hunters and eaters. So, in Grandpa's honor he decided to kill a lion and have a feast. Only the killing would be the chief displaying his bravery by killing the lion by himself with an ax! Grandpa drew me a picture. The ax was shaped like the axes of medieval times with the blade edge essentially a half round of a circle with the two points curving back to form the hammer shaped portion where it attaches to the handle which typically didn't exceed three feet long.

It began by the tribe singling out a lion. They circled it and each tribal member made noise, perhaps with some sort of tool. The circle closed in until the lion was trapped in the middle along with the chief. The lion roared and was angry. He swiped out at the chief with his front paw. The chief circled his ax at the paw, slicing it about 5" back. Infuriated, the lion crouched to initiate a leap upon the chief. The chief then stepped forward close to the lion. As the lion's head came forward, the chief buried the ax into the lion's forehead into his brain. The lion slumped over, back and died. The tribe hung him on a long wooden pole feet up and tied above and over the pole. They carried him back for butchering. They then had a big feast. Additional culinary delights are left to the imagination. Grandpa always said, "when in Rome......" After all, he grew up eating stinky cheese...he was conditioned!

He told me it was not difficult to get close to lions. They apparently were not overly afraid of humans, especially if they had recently eaten. A mother with cubs was a different story. Maybe that's why they say lions are king of the jungle!

He must have done some sightseeing while there, as best he could. Maybe this is where he obtained the ostrich egg souvenir he kept on the shelf at his home in Seattle.

It's unknown how long he stayed running that riverboat. Probably until he could catch another ship, head back and hire onto another. In any case it wasn't long. He wanted to keep moving.

***

It's unknown how he picked his ships hiring on anew. Perhaps it depended on the destination. But it appears he wanted more of North America and the United States, so he made it to the east coast.

My mother saved a picture of a ship called the Governor Robie that was featured in a Seattle newspaper on an unknown date, but most likely in the 1960's. She was a three masted full rigger first launched in Bath, Maine in 1883 registering 1,627 tons and for 15 years one of the fastest of her class. On the edge of the clipping is grandpa's writing where he says he made a trip... which means he hired on... from Baltimore to San Francisco which took 159 days. That equates to 5.3 months.

It would have been shorter via the Panama Canal, but alas even though its construction began in 1904, it was not completed until 1914.

So Lorenz's trips were around the southern tip of South America through either the Strait of Magellan, which precludes circling the actual Cape Horn which is Drake Passage. The Strait did save some time, but many sailing ships preferred Drake because of more favorable winds.

The Robie trip was one of those times. They hit a harrowing storm causing the ship to heal over. They took on water. Only the storm jibs were hurled. Lorenz lost some articles overboard. I have a framed mirror that Lorenz kept from the Robie. It's the one he had in the corner of his bathroom and would use when shaving.

His first postcard is dated May of 1904 from San Francisco. If he sailed there on the Governor Robie, he must have left around Thanksgiving of 1903. Since he had returned on the Errata a year prior, that gave him a year to get to Africa and then to the U.S east coast. He got around all right. Of course, I am piecing together these dates.

Really, 1904 is the beginning of the post cards. A photo of The Cliff House. It says, "Cliff House and Seal Rocks-San Francisco." In the foreground is the beach covered with patrons. But alas, there were no bikinis back then! Only men in suits and ladies in dresses. The publisher is Britton and Rey. It's in color. On the back it says Post Card. All the stamps of all his post cards have been removed.

In 1905 there are five postcards from:

1) California; Oil Steamer Atlas with Barge in Tow off Redondo.

2) Port Townsend, WA. People Dancing on a (giant) Tree Stump

3) WA. St. Indians getting ready for the Pow Wow.

4) Giant Fir Tree, near Seattle, loggers cutting.

5) Cedar Stump Residence. (Stump used as house)

Most are addressed to H. Laatz, his brother at Engelsgrube 80 in Lubeck, Germany. Also Mr. Burmester, his mother's second husband.

It's worth mentioning that this is when Lorenz's love for the northwest U.S. began, especially Puget Sound country with its mountains and forests. The tree postcards are of cedar and douglas fir ten to fifteen feet in diameter. There were Indian tribes still wearing their original garb. The sound was teaming with boats and ships. It must have been extremely exciting.

Back then, Port Townsend was a major port. It was at one time slated to be the capitol of Washington State but lost partially because of its tough railroad access. Its architecture was a clone of San Francisco, still evident today.

***

Oil Steamer Atlas With Her Barge In Tow At Redondo Cal.

1075—Dancing on Stump of Tree, Washington.
Copyright, 1904, by Lowman & Hanford S. & P. Co., Seattle.

GIANT FIR TREE, NEAR SEATTLE, WASHINGTON

205—GETTING READY FOR THE POW WOW.

1012--Cedar Stump Residence, Washington State.

Chapter 4:
The Pacific Ocean and Beyond

Leaving the northwest and its adventures behind, Lorenz must have been excited to leave the cold and go tropical. He was now a seasoned mariner and would be considered a top hand aboard ship. He wouldn't have a problem being hired. He knew navigation, knots, splices, sails, sail repair, macramé, and ship handling.

It must be mentioned that somewhere along the line he acquired carpentry skills and at some point, was considered the ship's carpenter. I still have the big box in which kept his collection of tools, and it still contains his wood planes, long bits for drilling holes in wood, a brace to drive the bits, chisels, etc. In the lid is a slotted rack for handsaws. I have a couple of those saws. His carpentry skills will be mentioned later when he reaches the Philippines.

There are three Hawaiian post cards. One is of hula dancers, dated 1908. The second is of a Royal Mausoleum, Honolulu, no date. The third is The Executive Building (formerly King's Palace), Honolulu, dated 1906. So he was there. My theory is he stopped going and again returning from the Philippines.

There are three cards from the P.I., all Manila. Only one is dated: 1908, A Family Pounding Rice. Another is:

Igorrotespackers, Benguet, P.I. The third: Government Laboratory, a beautiful building.

The Philippines was not a safe place. There were certain tribes that were revolutionaries or something. They would roam, attack and rob. Prior to arriving many on the crew were issued .38 caliber revolvers. I asked him if he had ever shot someone. He said no, if you aimed over their head and fired they would scatter.

Grandpa kept that pistol and would fire it on New Years Eve at midnight. He had blanks. I would stay up past my bedtime, eating cookies after dinner and watching TV. Then we would go to the back window which swung out on hinges like a door. He would wait until the clock struck midnight and then fire off a few rounds. The gunpowder really smelled awful.

Prior to landing in the Philippines, or maybe after they arrived, he the carpenter was given the task of making billy clubs for many of the crew. They were made from a very hard dark wood. Possibly mahogany. They shaped it like a small bat but with a shaped handle on the slim end. Each had a braided strap fashioned from white twine which was wrapped around the guard area and fastened with two nails. The strap was wrapped around the wrist and kept the club from slipping out of the hand. Back then, they had no lathes, so the club was shaped using a rasp. The wood was extremely hard and difficult to shape. He said they were in a rush to complete them so didn't get them perfectly round. I know his was not. He gave it to me before he died.

One time in the Philippines he and some friends were on liberty and encountered some thugs. For some reason a fight ensued. I don't think shots were fired. It was more of a club and fist fight. Evidently Lorenz and his mates prevailed. After it was over he saw a knife on the ground so he picked it up and saved it. That is 109 years ago.

He would bring it out and show it to me. After a time I would ask to see it. It had a water buffalo horn handle, a green color. The handle fit a small hand, as these people were small in size. The blade was so sharp, grandpa thought you could use it to shave. One day he said let's make a sheath, so we did, out of reddish colored leather. Then one day he gave it to me. I still have it. I wrapped and glued my high school graduation hat string with tassels around the open end. It is still sharp as a razor.

***

From the Philippine Islands, it appears the ship headed west.

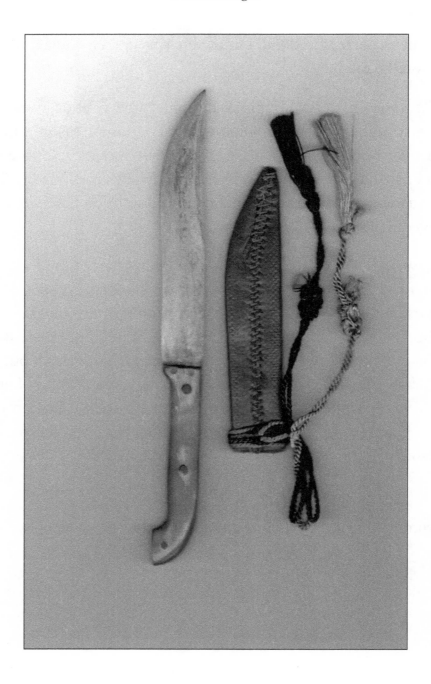

Chapter 5:
Adventures in Singapore

The Philippine Islands must have been a screaming adventure for a young Caucasian from Germany. The people, the food, the culture, and the hot humid climate was such a departure from anything Lorenz had seen. Of course, he had been to Africa which was similar.

But they did sail on toward Malaysia and pulled into Singapore, a major port, city-state and thriving metropolis. It was a unique multicultural experience and Lorenz must have been ecstatic to experience its diversity. He also paid a visit to the Raffles Hotel; this was a must; everyone did.

The Raffles opened in 1887 and was luxurious and lavish in its construction with nothing spared to insure its splendid unique flavor. A century later it was declared a National Monument and underwent a complete restoration at a cost of $160 million. All of its original colonial architecture was restored. It still stands today and considered one of the world's unique, special five-star hotels. But for Lorenz it was the site of an unpleasant adventure that he related to me. bib. 7

I assume they were in the bar. That's where sailors usually congregate. Words were said, personalities... maybe ethnicities... clashed and Lorenz was part of it. The next thing he knew, his adversary had grasped a liquor bottle by the neck, smashed it's bottom on the edge of the bar turning it into a cutting weapon and was coming at Lorenz. This would not, as they say, lead to a harmonious outcome. The odds didn't look good. So, Lorenz backed off and out toward the door, moving back to stay away. His attacker moved with him walking forward. When Lorenz saw an opening, he kicked as hard as he could. Where he struck, I do not know, but it was enough to stop the fellow's advance and not get cut. Maybe it was in a certain very sensitive male area. Anything is fair in self-defense, especially if it could mean your life! Lorenz then used his feet to get the hell out of there.... down the front steps and gone. Forget being too brave. And that's the way he related it to me. He never said if or when he returned to the Raffles.

I would love to go there and smoke a Cuban on the front steps.

After Singapore it looks like he sailed back east across the Pacific with stops along the way. He mentioned being in China, but I don't recall any specifics. By the postcard dates it appears he stopped once more in Hawaii in 1908.

Somewhere in his travels in the tropics he contracted malaria. In those days there were not many inoculations against diseases. After suffering through the original illness, later in life he would encounter flare-ups since malaria never leaves the body. Mother told about times growing up when he would get chills, fever, and the shakes.

He also contracted scurvy at some point in his travels. He still held resentment because an English ship refused to share some citrus fruit. Scurvy is caused by a lack of vitamin C.

The next postcard is dated 1908 and is people living in a cedar stump in Washington State and there are others of that area with no discernable dates. One is Cape Flattery which is the northwest tip of the state where the Pacific Ocean turns into the Strait of Juan de Fuca, which leads into Puget Sound, Port Townsend then Seattle. In German it says "around this rock we have to go in order to come to Seattle." There is one in color by Asahel Adams: "Seattle Puget Sound and the Olympic Mountains ", which may be dated 1912, it is not clear. One more is: "Music Stand, Golden Gate Park, San Francisco, California", dated 1912.

I have a photograph of Lorenz and another man standing on a log bridge. The writing on the back is my mother's. It says Woodland Park circa 1912. So he was around the west coast, Puget Sound and Alaska and down to California.

***

Grandpa had a knife he used as a letter opener with a handle he had fashioned from a deer antler. One day he explained how he got it. It seems one evening he was on liberty in some town somewhere and again they encountered some thugs assaulting a woman. He and his buddies laid into them. Lorenz engaged one particular fellow who came at him wielding a knife, thrusting downward in a stabbing motion. As the knife came, Lorenz laid a right cross on the man's jaw, most likely breaking it, because the guy went down. They then made a hasty retreat and returned to the ship. As he disrobed on the ship, removing his jacket, he discovered the dagger stuck into his shirt. Apparently, as contact was made with the man's jaw, the knife was let go and continued downward. Somehow years later the handle was lost or damaged, so Grandpa installed the antler piece. I still have that dagger and used it to open letters for years.

Seattle, Puget Sound and the Olympic Mountains.

A Sea Chanty by Lorenz A. Laatz

Twas on a cold and wintry night, the snow lay on the ground.
The sailor boy stood on the quay, the ship was outward bound.
His sweetheart standing by his side shed many a silent tear,
And as he pressed her to his heart, he whispered in her ear:

Farewell, farewell my own true love, this parting gives me pain.
You'll be my own, my guiding star, til I return again.
My thoughts will be with you my love, when storms are raging high.
So farewell love, remember me, your faithful sailor boy.

Then in the gale the ship set sail, the lass was standing by.
She watched the vessel out of sight, while tears bedimmed her eyes.
She prayed to God in heaven above, to guide him on his way.
Her lovers parting words the night reechoed over the bay.

Farewell, farewell my own true love, this parting gives me pain.
You'll be my own, my guiding star, til I return again.
My thoughts will be with you my love, when storms are raging high.
So farewell love, remember me, your faithful sailor boy.

So sad to say the ship returned without the sailor boy,
For he had died while on the sea, the flag was half mast high.
And when his comrades came ashore and told her he had died,
A letter which they gave to her, the last time sadly said:

Farewell, farewell my own true love, on earth we meet no more.
But we shall meet in heaven above, on that eternal shore.
I hope to see you in the land, in the land beyond the sky,
Where you shall no more part from me, your faithful sailor boy.

Chapter 6:
Switching from Sail to Steam

It's unclear just when Lorenz switched from sail to steam, only that he did. For sure, by 1909 on the west coast and up to Alaska, steamships had taken over. They were fueled by coal or oil, which heated a boiler producing steam, much like a train locomotive. The change had begun fifteen years earlier and grew at a rapid rate. So Lorenz experienced the transition of societal evolution and technology of the day.

It appears that Lorenz's trip to the western Pacific and on to Singapore were most likely on a steamship.

***

The Pacific Coast Steamship Company was an important early shipping company that operated steamships on the west coast of North America. Organized first in 1867 under the name of it's owners, but in 1876 took on the new name after buying out a competitor. They began with routes to 20 ports in California. Later on they expanded to the Pacific Northwest and on to Alaska, beginning about the time of the Klondike Gold Rush.

Some of their first steamers were side paddle construction. One such vessel the SS Pacific was lost off Cape Flattery, Washington with the deaths of over 200 people. Another, not a side paddle, The Valencia, ran aground onto the SW coast of

Vancouver Island after sailing north and missing the entrance to Juan de Fuca Strait because of fog. It was awful. Over 100 people, mostly women and children lost their lives.

By 1916, they were operating about 13 vessels when they sold to the Pacific Alaska Navigation Company, known as The Admiral Line, which had 9 vessels. The new name was the Pacific Steamship Company. That name was used until 1936 before operations ceased. bib. 8

***

In 1895, The Alaska Steamship Company was formed by Charles Peabody. It's first vessel was the 140 foot long Willapa which flew the historic Black Ball Flag which had originated on the east coast with trips to England and Europe. She carried passengers and freight making two trips a month to southeast Alaska competing with the Pacific Coast Steamship Company and others. His timing was perfect because in 1897 gold was discovered in the Klondike causing a fervor of activity and need for supplies to that area. 1898 was a frenzied year in shipping between Seattle and Alaska.

A rate war ensued as the Pacific Coast Steamship Company tried to stave off it's new rival. But apparently the newcomer was good at public relations, had capital backing and attracted patrons. The business grew, merged with and bought out others, thereby expanding. They also formed a new entity called the Puget Sound Navigation Company to service the inland waterways.

In 1903 they launched a new run from Seattle to Victoria with a 155 long vessel named the Clallam. It was a luxury ship with 44 staterooms. In 1904, they had to purchase three more vessels to keep up with the gold rush runs to Alaska. In 1906 they ferried he first automobile across the sound on the steamer State of Washington.

In 1908 the Puget Sound Navigation Company reorganized, increasing it's stock from $500,000 to $1.5 million. They eventually converted their fleet of Puget Sound vessels to carry autos, not just people. In 1918 they converted the Baily Gatzert into an auto ferry; in 1921 The City of Bremerton; in 1926 The Chippewa became the largest auto ferry on Puget Sound with the capacity for 90 cars and 2000 people. Folks called it The Black Ball Line. Their flag was red with a black ball in the middle. Later in 1935 arrived the famous Kalakala, whose design was Art Deco. This was the beginning of the present day Washington State Ferries.

In 1909, The Alaska Steamship Company sold out to the Alaska Syndicate who ran the ships mining copper in the Wrangell Mountains. bib. 9

***

After returning from the Western Pacific, Lorenz hired on with the Pacific Coast Steamship Company. He was now a ships officer: a mate. His runs were from Seattle to ports in British Columbia and Alaska. It must have been around 1909. His ships were hauling supplies, freight and people.

One adventure he related to me on his time between trips was a "tramp" from Port Angeles to Bremerton in Washington State. This route would take him through the Olympic Mountains. It is rugged terrain and to this day is not extensively traveled, especially compared to the Cascade Mountains. Again he wore some type of Indian moccasin, carried a 30-30 rifle and still had his .38 he was issued in the Philippines. He saw many wild animals and natural phenomena and partially lived off the land.

***

In December of 1909 Lorenz applied for American citizenship in Seattle. He had a Seattle address and stated he had resided in the United States for five years and Seattle for one. He is listed as 26 years old, white, blue eyes, brown hair, fair complexion and 5'-7" tall. Visible distinguishing marks are: "little finger missing on right hand." Nothing about tattoos. This may have necessitated some study and tests required for citizenship. The Certificate of Naturalization was issued on November 10, 2011. He was now officially an American. Did that give him dual citizenship? Maybe.

***

September 10, 1911 was an eventful day for Lorenz. He was working on the SS Northwestern enroute between Seattle and Alaska. It was more highly eventful for the 23 passengers and 52 crewmembers of the wooden passenger steamer SS Ramona, a sister ship owned by the Pacific Coast Steamship Co., carrying 405 tons of salmon and general cargo. She was traveling from Hunter Bay to Seattle when she hit the rocks of an unknown reef near Middle Spanish Island, Christian Sound, Alaska. The US Customs Wreck report says the conditions were: "light wind, swell, foggy and at night." bib. 10

It must be said the journey by sea between Seattle and Alaska was dangerous indeed. There were few aids to navigation such as buoys or light houses and no radar, GPS, LORAN and such which came later. Furthermore, the charts of the day were lacking relative to "underwater pinnacles" which were vertical outcroppings of rock which extended upward from the sea floor and were exacerbated by low tide. It was possible to pass over at high tide but not low tide. The water level varied from high tides of 14' to low tides of -4', which is a difference of 18'. During the change in tide there were eddies, swirls and strong currents. Combine that with strong winds, fog, and light and dark and it is a recipe for potential disaster. The waters of the Alaska coastline were littered with hundreds of wrecks. Reports say there have been several thousand total. bib. 11

Two other ships were in the vicinity: the SS Grand and the SS Delhi. The passengers and crew and 65% of the cargo was off loaded, but the Ramona was a total loss…sunk.

Lorenz had by now discovered cameras and loved taking pictures. He gave me his picture album, each page black heavy paper on which photos were glued. One complete page of the album has 6 pictures showing the rescue of passengers of the Ramona. One is an approaching lifeboat with folks aboard; another that life boat being hauled up on it's davits. The other four are of women and children on the Northwestern. On another page is a photo of Lorenz holding a laughing, rescued child. What's baffling is these photos are taken during daylight and the report says she went aground at night. Maybe the sun rose as the rescue ensued. For years after, some of the rescued stayed on touch with grandpa, forever grateful of his rescue efforts.

***

His camera was a small rectangular black box. He had pictures of many of the ships of his fleet, plus others. Here is a list of these ships in the photo album noted above:

SS Curacao (shown aground and braced on Fish Egg Isl. April/May 1913)

SS City of Seattle (aground and braced at Ketchikan, Alaska.)

SS Spokane (underway)

SS Ventura (underway)

SS Alameda (off Maude Island, Seymour Narrows)

SS State of California (underway)

Whaler Star (Wrangell Narrows)

SS Meteor (Ketchikan)

SS City of Seattle (aground and braced near Ketchikan, Alaska)

USS Manning (underway)

SS Weiding (underway)

SS Prince Rupert (underway)

Also in this picture album are numerous places and people in different parts of Alaska. Some are pictures of Lorenz aboard different ships on which he was working. These ships are: Curacao, Meteor, Spokane and Northwestern.

On June 30, 1911, the SS Spokane ran aground in Seymour Narrows. Crew and passengers survived and she was somehow refloated and repaired. The SS City of Seattle was wrecked on August 15, 1912. bib. 12

There is postcard dated January 10, 1912 from San Francisco of a music stand or stage, in Golden Gate Park. It is addressed to Burmeister in Lubeck. The address is 25 Fishergrube. This was to his mother's second husband.

Another postcard is from Prince Rupert, B.C., unreadable date, in color of an Indian cemetery in Hazelton, B.C.

***

Then came romance!

Grace Singer worked in a boarding house in Seattle very near or across from St. James Cathedral, a Catholic church. Lorenz must have stayed at the boarding house or had a friend that did. Grace had come from Leadville, Colorado with her mother and brother Fred after the death of their father.

They were of German heritage, and of course Lorenz was from Germany. Grace was ten years his junior, slim and beautiful. They hit it off. Fred liked Lorenz. He was a ship's officer.

There is a picture postcard of a steamer called the Meteor dated July 15, 1912, sent from Ketchikan, Alaska. It is from Lorenz, addressed to Miss Grace Singer. Lorenz writes: "Leave here this afternoon for Sulzer to load ore. From there straight to Seattle where we will be about July 20th. Best Greetings, Lorenz." He addresses exactly to that of St. James Cathedral. My guess is he didn't have her precise address and figured she would get it as the boarding house was close. Sulzer was a town in southeast Alaska named after William Sulzer, a miner of copper, hence the reference to ore.

Another postcard is of "Moonlight on Puget Sound", November of 1913, from Seattle, Washington, addressed to Lubeck, Germany. Beneath his greeting is Grace's writing and says: "Greetings from Grace Singer". They were a couple. He was her sailor boy and was 30 years old.

There's a postcard addressed to Mr. Burmeister in Lubeck, Germany dated April 16, 1914. It's a color photo of the St. James Cathedral in Seattle. Lorenz writes: "This is the cathedral where we got married." Lorenz and Grace were married the previous day on April 15.

***

On Saturday June 21, 1913, the 241' iron steamer SS Curacao struck an uncharted rock 1.5 miles WSW of Culebra Island Tonowak Bay and was lost. The time was 0720. Not a good breakfast that morning! 39 passengers and 51 crew were transported from the wreck by the USCG SS Gedney to Ketchikan. She was carrying 1200 tons of cargo. Her owner was the Pacific Coast Steamship Company. Her Master was William Thompson of Seattle. bib. 13

Grandpa's photo album has a nice photo of Bill Thompson. Also some shots of Lorenz and Grace standing with some of the crew. Another of an unknown lady aboard the Curacao. One is of Lorenz standing on deck by himself. All taken when Lorenz was a member of her crew.

Then there are four photos of the Curacao beached for 5 days on Fish Egg Island from May 25th to May1st ostensibly to work on her hull or simply clean it.

But the kicker is the series of photos of her after striking the rocks and then sinking in stages. His writing is in white ink on the black album paper. It says: "SS Curacao struck Peter Rock in Cold Chuck Bay Hecata Isl. 7:30 AM, June 21, 1913." It shows lifeboats departing; then "5 min. before going down"; then "15 min after going down" with only her stack showing. Then a shot taken from the cannery nearby. There is a photo of the afterdeck of the Curacao showing chunks of marble. He also had a post card entitled "last boat leaving the Curacao" in with the other photos.

He must not have been on the Curacao when she wrecked and I don't recall him discussing it. If he was not aboard, he must have been nearby, because these photos were taken by him and developed. It appears he was on the Northwestern because the photo was taken from that ship.

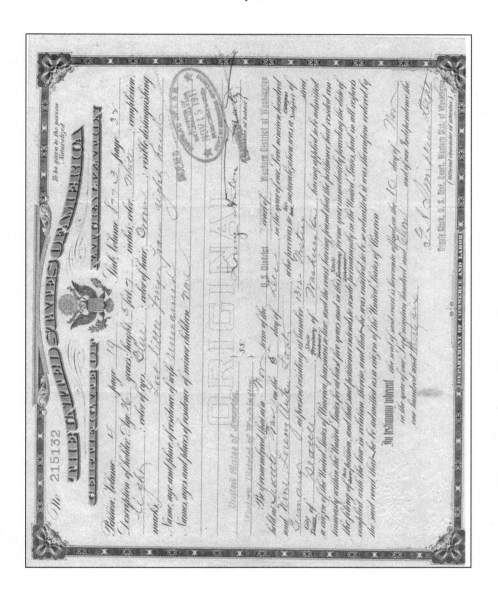

Wreck of ½ Ramona. Spanish Isl.

Bill Thompson.

S/S Meteor in Seaway

2417 Prescott Ave. SW.
Seattle, Wash.
November 24 1935

Mr. L.A.Laatz,
4103 38th. Ave. So.
Seattle, Wash.

My dear Sir:

       With reference to a very pleasant talk
I had with you in my office not long a go and our
discussion of the wreck of the RAMONA I am enclosing
herewith two snap shots of the baby for whom you made
the blanket suit and the little cap decorated with sea-
grass on that memorable event. Due to the good care that
baby got he has turned out to be a strong healthy young
man and is on his way to be an Admiral USN.

       These two pictures taken the day he grad-
uated from Annapolis with the class of 1933 are all I
have. He was married last August and is on duty at
Pearl Harbor, Hawaii.

       Mrs. Derickson was very much pleased to
hear of you again and joins me in sending our very best
regards to you and your family.

            Very truly yours,

            R.B.Derickson,

Last boat off the sinking Curacao.

Boarding House, Seattle

Chapter 7:
Life After the Sea

The last postcard is the one sent the day before his marriage to Grace of St. James Cathedral. After that, he mailed to Germany photos he took with his camera along with notes. He did that for years and always stayed in touch with family in his birth country. Years later his oldest daughter Frances took over.

Lorenz and Grace bought a house in south Seattle and on February 1, 1916 they had their first child, Frances Mary, my mother. They had four more children including one boy named Lorenz. It was a tiny house for that many to be raised, but they did it.

The big story though was Lorenz giving up his life working on the water. Apparently his mother in law was a large influence in this decision, citing his absence on trips along with the danger involved since there were so many shipwrecks. He acquiesced, but was now faced with changing from a profession he had been honing for 12 years and was highly accomplished to something else altogether new. He truly loved the sea and life on the water. What a shame! Some years later the decision reared it's ugly head when in 1929 the economy collapsed into The Great Depression. It proved a financial family hardship. If he had stayed on the water, life for him and his family would have been much different. They were poor.

Lorenz's new profession would be that of an electrician. He studied some courses and learned the trade. He also did some peripheral construction work.

In February of 1915, he joined The Sons of Hermann, a German fraternal organization. The cost to join was $500 and enjoined Washington State and British Columbia. He had not yet left working on the water. Later on he would bring Frances with him to some of his meetings. They celebrated German heritage and customs eating German food including stinky cheese. Frances loved to write growing up and would correspond with relatives in the old country. Things were slightly tense in 1918 with the breakout of WWI in Germany. America was somewhat worried about German spies, but Lorenz was an established citizen with a family. Plus he had the tattoo of the American flag on his arm with an eagle!

And there is where my story ends because it is about him working on the sea, traveling the world and the stories he related to me of that time. Grandpa was 61 years old when I was born. He lived until age 79 and I was 16. The night he died I had gone to bed and had a dream that something was wrong with him, a premonition. My parents woke me saying he was ill and we must go to his house. He died that night.

Lorenz Anton Ludwig Laatz was a strong, stubborn, intelligent man...very talented. Very German, but all American. He lived a long exciting life and passed his genes and strong male values onto his offspring.

I am blessed to have spent time with him, shared his love and heard his stories as he related them. I in turn have done my best relating them to you.

Epilogue

It should be said that around the years 1907-1910 Lorenz sent postcards to Lubeck from the gold fields of the Yukon where he spent some time mining. It wasn't a long or significant period however and I don't recall any notable stories. (see postcards) This was probably prior to meeting Grace and becoming enamored.

He did relate a hike overland from Anchorage to Fairbanks which he called "a tramp." He had a friend, a Frenchman, who went with him. They observed all nature had to offer in wild Alaska.

In May of 1958 at age 75 Lorenz wrote this poem:

Oh Lubeck, the town where I was born
My love for you has never worn.
Though my allegiance has changed,
My heart is where in youth I ranged.

Bibliography

#1 Lubeck; from Wikipedia, the free encyclopedia; online. 5/28/2012. History, references, external links. en.m.wikipedia.org

#2 Ibid

#3 Ibid

#4 Ibid

#5 Ibid

#6 online World Health Organization. who.int Yellow Fever.

#7 Wikipedia. Raffles Hotel History en,m.wikipedia.org

#8 Wikipedia. Pacific Coast Steamship Co. history, references, external links.

#9 Wikipedia. Pacific-Alaska Steamship Co. References.

#10 www.wrecksite.eu Ramona. Alaskashipwrecks.com/shipwrecks-a-z

#11 ibid

#12 ibid SS City of Seattle wreck

#13 ibid SS Curacao

CPSIA information can be obtained
at www.ICGtesting.com
Printed in the USA
LVHW092114251121
704451LV00006B/473